TO DEAR DAD ENJOY LOVE YAS

ALSO BY

MARIANNE WILLIAMSON

A Return to Love

A Woman's Worth

Illuminata

Emma and Mommy Talk to God

The Healing of America

Marianne Williamson

Illuminated Prayers

*Watercolors
by Claudia Karabaic Sargent*

Simon & Schuster

SIMON & SCHUSTER
Rockefeller Center
1230 Avenue of the Americas
New York, NY 10020

Text copyright © 1997 by Marianne Williamson
Illustrations copyright © 1997 by Claudia Karabaic Sargent
All rights reserved,
including the right of reproduction
in whole or in part in any form.

SIMON & SCHUSTER and colophon are registered trademarks
of Simon & Schuster Inc.

Designed by Karolina Harris

Manufactured in the United States of America

1 3 5 7 9 10 8 6 4 2

Library of Congress Cataloging-in-Publication Data is available.

· ISBN 0-684-84483-4

hope *Illuminated Prayers* will be a comforting companion for those who read it. Many times my spirits have been lifted by something I found in a small spiritual volume, something I could throw in my purse and then count on to bring me back to serenity as I sat in a doctor's waiting room, stood in line at the DMV, or sat up in bed at the end of a long day. I think of prayer as a spiritual lifeline back to where I most want to be.

With that in mind, I send these prayers out into the world. I hope that they provide some solace and happiness to those who read them and utter them and feel them. They did that for me as I wrote them.

Marianne Williamson

Illuminated
Prayers

$\mathcal{D}$ EAR $\mathcal{G}$ OD,

As I wake up this morning

may Your spirit come upon me.

May my mind receive

Your emanations,

my soul receive

Your blessing,

and my heart receive

Your love.

May all those I meet

or even think of on this day

feel better for it.

May I contribute peace.

May I serve Your purposes

with all I say and do,

today and always.

Please show me how.

$\mathcal{A}$ MEN

DEAR GOD,

here my body is broken,

please heal it.

May every cell

be filled with grace

and returned to its

divine right placement,

in me

and in all others.

AMEN

DEAR GOD,

May my body be
a temple to Your spirit.
May every cell
be filled with light,
the radiance
of You.

May my mouth speak
only
what You would have me say.
May my legs walk
only
in the directions You would will.

May my hands
carry forth Your work
in all I say
and do.

May health be mine.
May all disease
depart
from me
and everyone.

In the name of God,
may the forces of sickness
leave
the bodies of His children,
never to return.

$\mathcal{A}$ MEN

DEAR GOD,

y body is broken,

I need Your help.

I fear I will not get well.

Please God,

send angels to deliver me from my pain

and sickness

and fear,

now.

I know salvation is the only true Cure,

and yet I doubt

when my body hurts.

Help me, Lord.

Please bless my medicine

and guide my healers.

Thank you, God.

$\mathcal{A}$ M E N

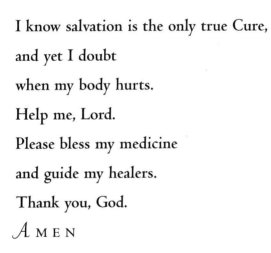

DEAR GOD,

lease send to me

the spirit of Your peace.

Then send,

dear Lord,

the spirit of peace

from me

to all the world.

May everyone I think of

and all who think of me

see only innocence

and love—

for that is who
we are.

Bless,
dear God,
my bond with others.
Make holy my relationships
and peaceful
our communications,
body to body
and
soul to soul.
Amen

DEAR GOD,

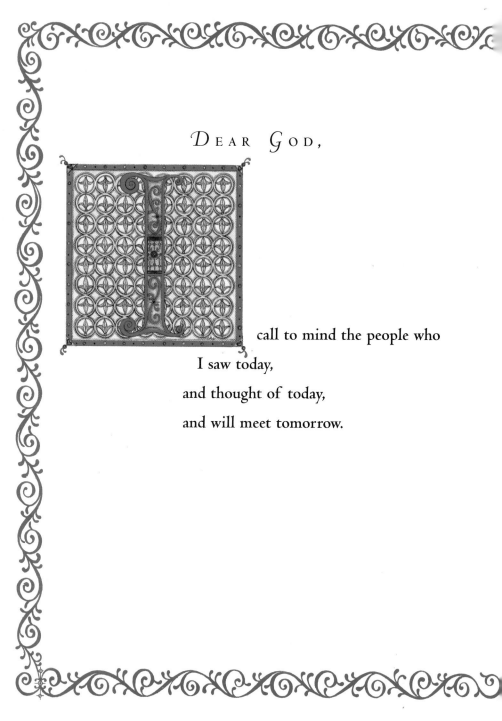

I call to mind the people who

I saw today,

and thought of today,

and will meet tomorrow.

I surrender them to You.

Please bless each one,

and gladden each one,

and heal each one.

A M E N

DEAR GOD,

hen I perceive

my brothers' faults,

please transform my perceptions.

May I see only innocence,

for that is where You are.

When I am tempted

to forget

the truth

of who my sister is,

may I see only innocence,

for that is who You are.

When I am tempted to forget

that I am only love—

may I see only innocence,

for that is what You are.

$\mathcal{A}$ M E N

DEAR GOD,

 call to mind
the people I will see today.
Please bless them all.

May everyone in the world
find peace today—
each and every man
each and every woman
each and every child—
may all of them be blessed.

May the world
retrieve its purpose,
the divinity of its mission,
to reflect and glorify
Your love
forever.

$\mathcal{A}$ M E N

DEAR GOD,

lease bless this marriage.

May the presence of

the Holy Spirit

come upon us

and sweetly crown our union.

May he see in me,

and I see in him,

28

the mystery of Heaven.

May our joys be deep

and our wounds be sacred.

Post angels to protect us, Lord,

from the demons that would

divide our hearts.

Now and forever.

$\mathcal{A}$ M E N

DEAR GOD,

lease break the
unhealthy bond
which keeps me tied
where I should not be tied.
Separate who should be separate,
Lord,

that I might dwell

without brokenness

to one

who is broken.

A M E N

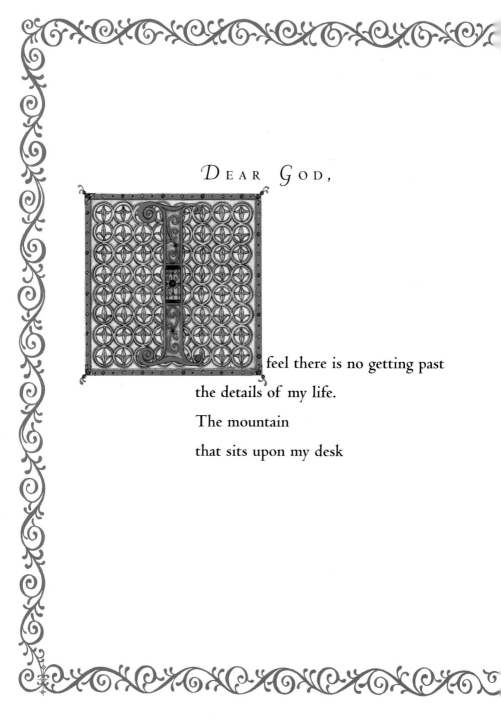

D EAR G OD,

feel there is no getting past
the details of my life.

The mountain

that sits upon my desk

now sits

upon my heart.

Clean both,

dear God.

$\mathcal{A}$ M E N

D EAR G OD,

ay the gap which separates

earth from Heaven

close.

I surrender

my focus

on my brother's guilt,

my focus on his errors,

my instinct to condemn.

ear God,

please teach me

forgiveness.

Release us both from hell.

$\mathcal{A}$ MEN

DEAR GOD,

May the walls
which keep me separate—
from my brothers,
my sisters,
my self,
and You—
now melt.

May the thoughts
and feelings
which keep me in hell,
be dissolved
forever.
𝒜 M E N

DEAR GOD,

The world is so unsure,

I know not where to find

the safety that I seek.

I fear

when I observe the horrors

and the violence of the world.

I pray for those

now caught in it—

I pray that I might never be—

I pray for all the children,

that the darkness

coming at the world

might be turned back

and sent away

to the nothingness

from whence it came.

Lord grant me power,

that I might command the darkness—

in the name of God,

and the Holy Spirit—

 o now,

we say,

to violence

and evil

and all variety

of darkness,

go away from earth,

disembark our planet,

leave our minds

and abandon our streets,

for we claim them all

for God,

for love,

for peace.

I command you now,

in the name of God,

get away from our children,

get out of our hearts,

and do not return.

For we proclaim

the name of God,

and claim this planet for the

forces of His love.

𝒜 M E N

DEAR GOD,

Please bless
the children of earth,
mine and all others,
the precious angels in our midst.
Send all darkness away from them.
Thank you, God.
AMEN

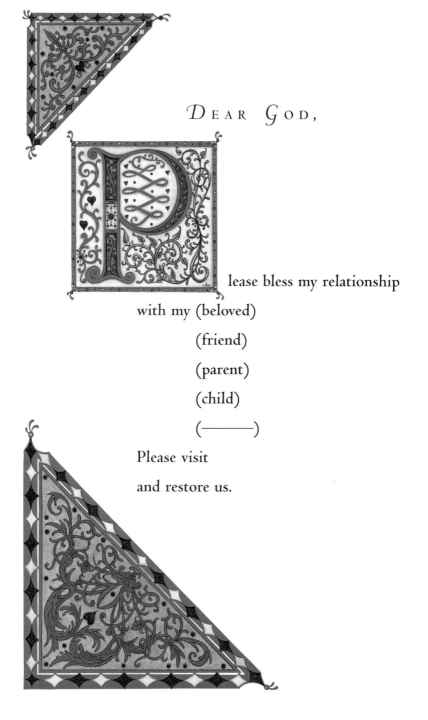

D EAR G OD,

P lease bless my relationship
with my (beloved)
(friend)
(parent)
(child)
(———)
Please visit
and restore us.

Please bring us both

to peace.

Melt down the walls between us,

and free us from the limits

that the walls

imposed upon us.

 less us both.

$\mathcal{A}$ M E N

DEAR GOD,

May there come
over the earth
a great and glorious
light.
May we remember eaven.

May all who suffer
feel pain no more.
May sorrow depart,
may disease end,
may war stop,
may doubts cease,

and all hearts
gladden.
May we remember eaven.

May every child
and every man
and every woman
now, this instant,
feel sure release
from the bondage of their past.
$\mathcal{A}$ M E N

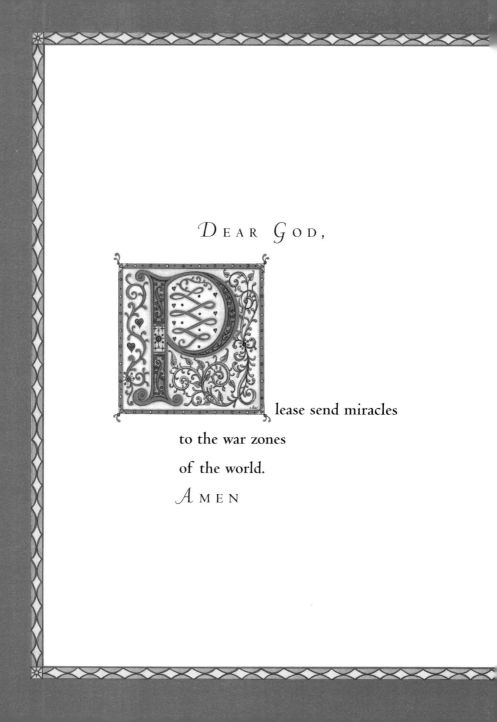

DEAR GOD,

Please send miracles
to the war zones
of the world.
AMEN

DEAR GOD,

Please help the children
of this world.

hey are hurt and hurting
and are crushed beneath the weight
of our insanity.
Please bless the children,
and awaken us
before it is too late.

AMEN

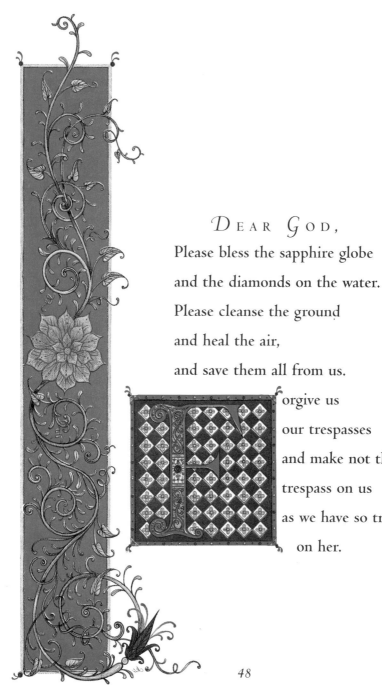

D E A R   G O D ,

Please bless the sapphire globe

and the diamonds on the water.

Please cleanse the ground

and heal the air,

and save them all from us.

orgive us

our trespasses

and make not the earth

trespass on us

as we have so trespassed

on her.

ave mercy on us,

and on her,

and heal our broken bond.

$\mathcal{A}$ M E N

DEAR GOD,

ay miracles

replace war,

May miracles

replace hatred,

May miracles

replace judgment,

May miracles
replace fear,
in me
and in the world.
$\mathcal{A}$ M E N

D EAR G OD,

ay the sky be cleansed

May the waters be cleansed

May the ground be cleansed

May our hearts be cleansed

May our minds be cleansed

and thus made new.

$\mathcal{A}$ M E N

D EAR G OD,

M ay the world transform

as in a blazing fire,

and I,

oh Lord,

along with it.

A MEN

DEAR GOD,

 give to you this morning.

Please break the chain

with yesterday

and free my life to greater things.

AMEN

D EAR G OD,

lease bless our home,

the earth

wherein we dwell.

There are those who suffer here,

and know not what to do.

There are those who fear their lot,

and know not where to go.

eal them all,

dear God,

and bring them out of darkness

into light.

$\mathcal{A}$ MEN

DEAR GOD,

I give to you this night.

Post angels round my home,

my bed,

my children,

my loves,

and everyone.

Send angels through the world tonight,

to heal the sick

and awaken the dead.

et miracles
replace the pain
in all of us.
Lay Your hands on all our eyes,
that we might see
at last.

A M E N

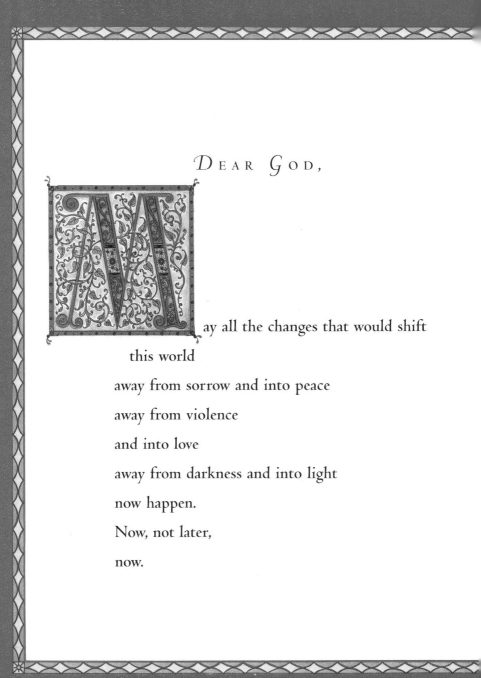

D E A R   G O D,

ay all the changes that would shift

this world

away from sorrow and into peace

away from violence

and into love

away from darkness and into light

now happen.

Now, not later,

now.

May a great and glorious light

emerge

and show us all

the way.

May our eyes look up at an illumined sky

and see a sign

that means

have hope

and pray,

for the Lord has found His way to you.

 ow, not later,

now.

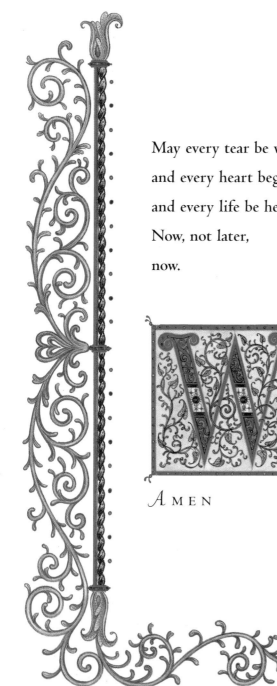

May every tear be wiped away
and every heart begin to gladden
and every life be healed by love.
Now, not later,
now.

We pray
and say thanks,
for we are heard.
He hears us.
Now, not later,
now.

A M E N

DEAR GOD,

ay every aspect of my being

be converted into Truth.

May every cell fall into place

and serve a higher plan.

I no longer wish to be

who I was.

wish for more.

AMEN

DEAR GOD,

ay my heart
become my only perceiver
and my eyes be full of light.

May angels' wings
be lent to me,
that I might fly
above the noise
and turmoil
of the world.

ith every moment's flight

may something beautiful

be revealed to me,

and become a part

of who I am.

A M E N

DEAR GOD,

May the diamond center

of my love

shine forth

to magnify

Your light.

May my love

not be hidden

from me

or from others.

May You

come forth

in who I am

that

I am.

$\mathcal{A}$ MEN

D EAR G OD,

The world is like a veil
across my eyes.
I cannot see.
Please remove the veil, dear God,
and let me see beyond it.
Deliver me to peace.

emove the scales that hide from me

the love

in every thing.

$\mathcal{A}$ MEN

D EAR G OD,

here are places in me

where I am broken.

Please touch my heart

and heal me.

Thank you, God.

A M E N

D EAR G OD ,

 ay all my ideas be of You.

May all my perceptions be of You.

May all my feelings be of You.

And You alone.

A MEN

DEAR GOD,

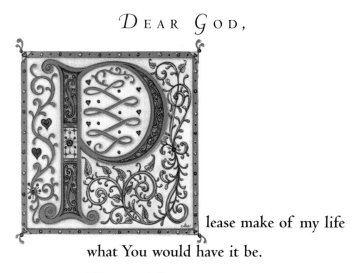

lease make of my life
what You would have it be.
Time and fate
have twisted things
I cannot straighten out
alone.
Dear God,
may I begin again.

My body

my mind

my spirit

my love

my hate

my pain

my sorrows

my joy

my questions

my fears

my hopes

my visions

I give them all

to You.

$\mathcal{A}$ M E N

DEAR GOD,

If it is Your will,

may I please have

the happiness I dream of.

All of it,

according to Your will,

now and forever.

Thank you, God.

AMEN

DEAR GOD,

cannot describe in words
the misery I feel.
But you know.
Please enter my heart
transform my thoughts
make straight my way
and set me free.
Thank you, God.
AMEN

DEAR GOD,

lease help me.

I can sense the beauty of Heaven

and the peace of Your arms,

but I cannot find them

here.

May I come home while still on earth?

Please take me there, and keep me.

Thank you, God.

AMEN

DEAR GOD,

ay my gifts

begin to blossom

in a way that serves Your plan.

AMEN

77

DEAR GOD,

Please lift the veil

that separates me

from the Heaven which lay beyond.

Renew my thoughts

so full of fear and judgment and the illusions

   of the world

Renew my heart

so burdened by the sorrows of the past

Renew my hopes

o often squelched.

send angels, God,

to sit with me and walk with me

and whisper in my ears.

May I be

here for You

and here with You

and see You in all things.

Please help me see the innocence of life.

A M E N

DEAR GOD,

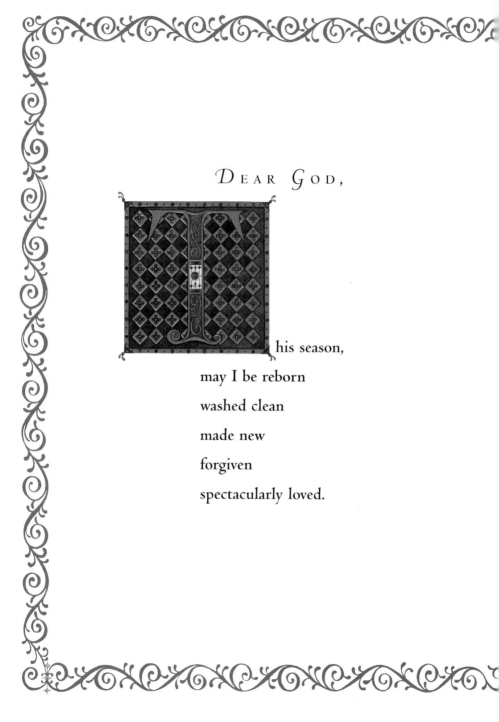

This season,

may I be reborn

washed clean

made new

forgiven

spectacularly loved.

emind me who I am.

Forgive me for my shadow sides,

please heal my broken wings

that I might fly

with You.

$\mathcal{A}$ M E N

DEAR GOD,

May all the tears I cry, and all the

tears

I have not cried

but hold within,

pour forth into Your hands.

Please take each painful thought
and unhealed wound,
and send Your angels
here
to me.
I long for peace.
A M E N

DEAR GOD,

Please sew my heart back together. AMEN

D EAR G OD,

 he memories that haunt

me now

please take away

forever.

A MEN

D E A R G O D ,

Please forgive me my

errors.

I surrender now

my shame,

my guilt,

the wrongs which I have done.

I am so sorry.

I atone.

I go back,

dear Lord,

to the moment of disruption.

I give to You

that moment.

Please give new life

to me.

orgive me,

and teach me how to forgive

myself

and others.

$\mathcal{A}$ M E N

DEAR GOD,

May hatred be forever

banished

from the universe.

In the name of God,

may hatred cease.

Make my heart a harmless,

peaceful place.

AMEN

D EAR G OD,

May the stars

which fill the sky

fill me.

A MEN

DEAR GOD,
May I cross over now
from boy to man,
(from girl to woman)
from child to adult
at last.
AMEN

DEAR GOD,

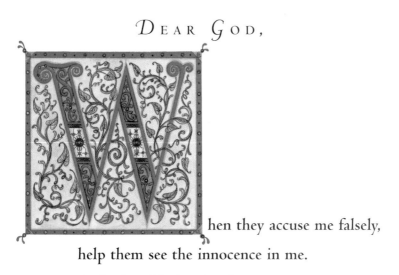

hen they accuse me falsely,

help them see the innocence in me.

And when I judge, Lord,

help me see the innocence in them.

AMEN

D EAR G OD,

Please help me dedicate

myself to You—

to do the work,

to quiet my mind,

that I might serve You best.

Please introduce my heart
to peace,
and guide me to the chamber
where my heart
can rest
and find itself.
Please take me there.

$\mathcal{A}$ M E N

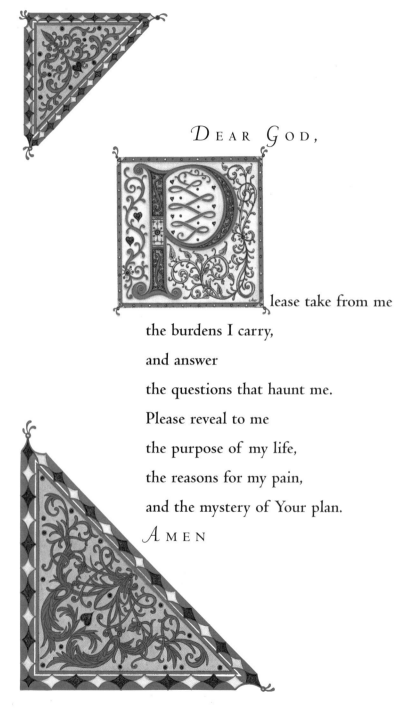

DEAR GOD,

Please take from me

the burdens I carry,

and answer

the questions that haunt me.

Please reveal to me

the purpose of my life,

the reasons for my pain,

and the mystery of Your plan.

AMEN

DEAR GOD,

Please take away
my inappropriate
desires.
Please release me
from my cravings.
Replace them all
with You.
AMEN

DEAR GOD,

lease help me to detach

from things that hold me back.

Remove from me

illusions and falsehood.

Restore to me

the lightness

of my being.

AMEN

D E A R G O D,

lease bless the ones

who have no hope,

and show me how to help.

A M E N

DEAR GOD,

Please bless my mother and

father

my teachers and healers

my friends and lovers

my children and theirs.

AMEN

Dear God,

Please mend my broken relationships

for I do not know how.

how me their innocence

and please show them mine.

Thank you, Lord.

Amen

DEAR GOD,

Please bless my country

and every country.

Forgive this century

its violence and pain,

and bless the century now upon us.

AMEN

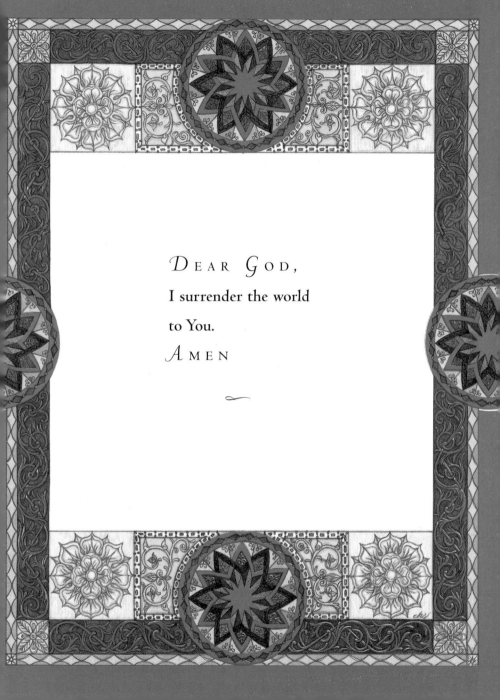

DEAR GOD,
I surrender the world
to You.
AMEN

About the Author

Marianne Williamson is the best-selling author of *A Return to Love*, *A Woman's Worth*, *Illuminata*, and *The Healing of America*. She is also the author of a children's book, *Emma and Mommy Talk to God*.